SIKH
Prayer and Worship

Rajinder Singh Panesar/Anita Ganeri

SEA-TO-SEA
Mankato Collingwood London

This edition first published in 2008 by
Sea-to-Sea Publications
1980 Lookout Drive
North Mankato
Minnesota 56003

Printed in China

Library of Congress Cataloging in Publication Data

Panesar, Rajinder Singh.
    Sikh prayer and worship / by Rajinder Singh Panesar and Anita Ganeri.
        p.cm. -- (Prayer and worship)
    Includes bibliographical references and index.
    ISBN 978-1-59771-094-7
    1. Prayer--Sikhism--Juvenile literature. 2. Worship (Sikhism)--Juvenile literature.
    I. Ganeri, Anita, 1961- II. Title

BL2018.42.P36 2007
294.6'43--dc22

                                                              2006051291

9 8 7 6 5 4 3 2

Published by arrangement with the Watts Publishing Group Ltd, London.

Editor: Rachel Cooke
Design: Joelle Wheelwright
Picture research: Diana Morris

Acknowledgments:
Chris Fairclough/Franklin Watts: 8, 18, 21. Hutchison/Eye Ubiquitous: front cover b, 29. Jenny Matthews/Franklin
Watts: 6, 19. Richard T. Nowitz/Corbis: 5.
Christine Osborne/World Religions Photo Library: front cover c, 26. Rajinder Singh Panesar: 9, 11, 12, 14, 15,
16, 20. Helene Rogers/Ark Religion: 10, 13, 22, 25, 27.
Steve Shott/Franklin Watts: 7, 17, 23, 28. Liba Taylor/Hutchison/Eye Ubiquitous: 24.

Every attempt has been made to clear copyright. Should there be any inadvertent omission please apply to the
publisher for rectification.

*This Sikh symbol is called the Khanda.
The double-edged sword at its center
represents the one creative power of God
above the universe.*

Contents

The prayers in this book were chosen by Rajinder Singh Panesar. Rajinder is a practicing Sikh who works for the Bradford Interfaith Education Center as a Sikh faith tutor. Rajinder also teaches Sikhism and Punjabi language in schools, colleges, and gurdwaras. He is involved in many gurdwaras and other Sikh organizations both locally, in West Yorkshire, and nationally, around the UK.

About Sikhism

Sikhs are followers of a religion called Sikhism, which began about 500 years ago in the Punjab region of northwestern India. At that time, the main religions in India were Hinduism and Islam but there were many conflicts between the two. A holy man, called Nanak (1469–1539), introduced a new religion that taught equality and tolerance. He became the first of the ten Sikh Gurus, or holy teachers.

This is the symbol of Ik Onkar, which means "one God."

Sikh beliefs

Sikhs believe in Ik Onkar which means "one God." They believe God exists in everyone and everything in the universe, and that, therefore, everyone and everything is equal. Sikhs hope to grow closer to God by remembering God in everything they do. This makes praying to and praising God an essential part of a Sikh's life.

There is only one God and God is the only truth. God the creator is without fear, without hate, and immortal. God is beyond death and is understood through God's grace.

About this prayer

This is the first verse of the Mool Mantar which means "basic teaching." The prayer forms the first paragraph of the Guru Granth Sahib, the Sikhs' holy book (see page 7). It sums up what Sikhs believe about God. God cannot be seen but is always present and everywhere. God was not born and will not die.

Three golden rules

Sikhs also follow three golden rules which were given to them by Guru Nanak. These are:

1) Nam japna: Meditating on God's name. Praying to and thinking about God is very important. Guru Nanak said that when people pray to God, it is the only time their minds have a chance to rest.

2) Kirat karna: Earning an honest living. Working hard is part of being a Sikh. Guru Nanak said that if Sikhs feed their families with money earned in a dishonest way, their children may grow up to be bad people.

3) Vand chhakna: Sharing our time and earnings with needy people.
Guru Nanak instructed Sikhs to share 10 percent of their earnings with needy people and to spend 10 percent of their time working for good causes.

Sikhs around the world

Today there are about 14 million Sikhs. Most still live in India but through emigration, strong Sikh communities have grown up in the UK, Canada, Australia, and the USA.

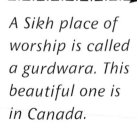

A Sikh place of worship is called a gurdwara. This beautiful one is in Canada.

Sikh Prayer and Worship

For Sikhs, saying prayers is a way of spending time in God's company. Even though they cannot see God, they feel able to pray to God as a caring friend. Some Sikhs like to visit a gurdwara, the Sikh place of worship, to pray in the presence of the Guru Granth Sahib, the holy book. Most Sikhs also worship at home.

Sikh prayers

There are two kinds of Sikh prayers. The first kind is set prayers which Sikhs say every day at home or in the gurdwara, in the morning, evening, and before going to sleep. These prayers are called Nit nem (see page 10). The second kind is personal prayers, which Sikhs can say anywhere and at any time. Sikh prayers may be read or sung as songs. They are said in the Punjabi language and written down in Gurmukhi script.

A boy says his evening prayers before going to sleep. When Sikhs pray they usually close their eyes and put the palms of their hands together.

The Guru Granth Sahib

Most Sikh prayers come from the Guru Granth Sahib, the holy book of the Sikhs. When the tenth Sikh Guru, Gobind Singh (1666–1708) was dying, he did not name a person to succeed him as Guru. Instead, he said that the Guru Granth Sahib should be the Sikh's everlasting guide. The Guru Granth Sahib is a collection of hymns and verses, written by Guru Nanak and five of the other Gurus, together with Hindu and Muslim holy men. Prayers also come from the Dasam Granth, a collection of hymns by Guru Gobind Singh, and from the songs of a Sikh scholar called Bhai Gurdas (c.1551–1637).

Sikhs treat the Guru Granth Sahib with great respect as they believe it contains the word of God, passed on by the Gurus.

Blessed is the hour when I see You.
I am glad to be in Your presence.
You are the giver of my life,
my beloved God;
I maintain my whole being by
keeping You in mind.
Your teaching is true,
Your word is sweet,
Your eyes see everything,
You are calmness itself.
Your patience is the
source of my peace,
Your law is unchanging, my Lord.
My God is beyond birth and death.

About this prayer

This is a prayer from the Guru Granth Sahib, which is recited when a copy of the Guru Granth Sahib is installed in a gurdwara or in a Sikh's home. It was written by the fifth Sikh Guru, Arjan (1536–1606). After the prayer is said, everyone bows and sits down. A granthi (see page 9) then reads from the Guru Granth Sahib. For some Sikhs, it is as though their Guru is whispering words of wisdom in their ears.

Bedtime prayers

The final set prayer of the day is called the Kirtan Sohila. It is recited at night before you go to sleep. For this reason, it is not a very long prayer because people may be tired. The purpose of the prayer is to turn your mind away from the cares and concerns of the day to focus on God.

Hymn of joy

Kirtan Sohila means "hymn of joy." This prayer is actually made up of five hymns. Three were composed by Guru Nanak; one by the fourth Guru, Ram Das (1534-1581), and one by Guru Arjan. Apart from at bedtime, this prayer is also recited when a person dies (see pages 24–25). Through the prayer, Sikhs ask God for the courage and strength to face discomfort and death. It is believed that those who say this prayer sincerely will not be afraid of death. It is also recited in the gurdwara when the copy of the Guru Granth Sahib is put to rest at the end of the day.

Bedtime prayers help Sikhs to leave behind the worries of the day.

When we are gathered to worship the Master,
Sing to His praises and ponder His name.
Sing to His glory, reflect on His wonders,
He who is Lord and Creator of all.
Sing to His praises, our Lord who is fearless.
Humbly, I bow for the song which brings joy.
He who gives life is our constant Protector,
Watching and guarding us, safe in His care.
How can we judge all His goodness and mercies,
How grasp the worth of His marvelous grace?
God has determined the time for my nuptials,
Come pour the oil of joy at my door.
Bless me, my friends, that I find this sweet union,
Dwelling as one with my Master and Lord.
All must receive their last call from the Master,
Daily He summons those souls who must go.
Hold in remembrance the Lord who will summon you.
Soon you will hear His command.

About this prayer

This is the first hymn of the Kirtan Sohila prayer. It was composed by Guru Nanak. Through this hymn, Sikhs remember God as powerful and fearless. They ask Him for protection, as their master and provider of countless blessings. Since God has decided on everyone's last day on Earth, Sikhs request their friends to pray for them and give them good wishes so that they can unite with God as in a marriage (nuptials). This union with God is something all Sikhs hope for.

After a bedtime story, grandparents often recite the Kirtan Sohila to their grandchildren so that the children do not have nightmares.

Birthday Prayers

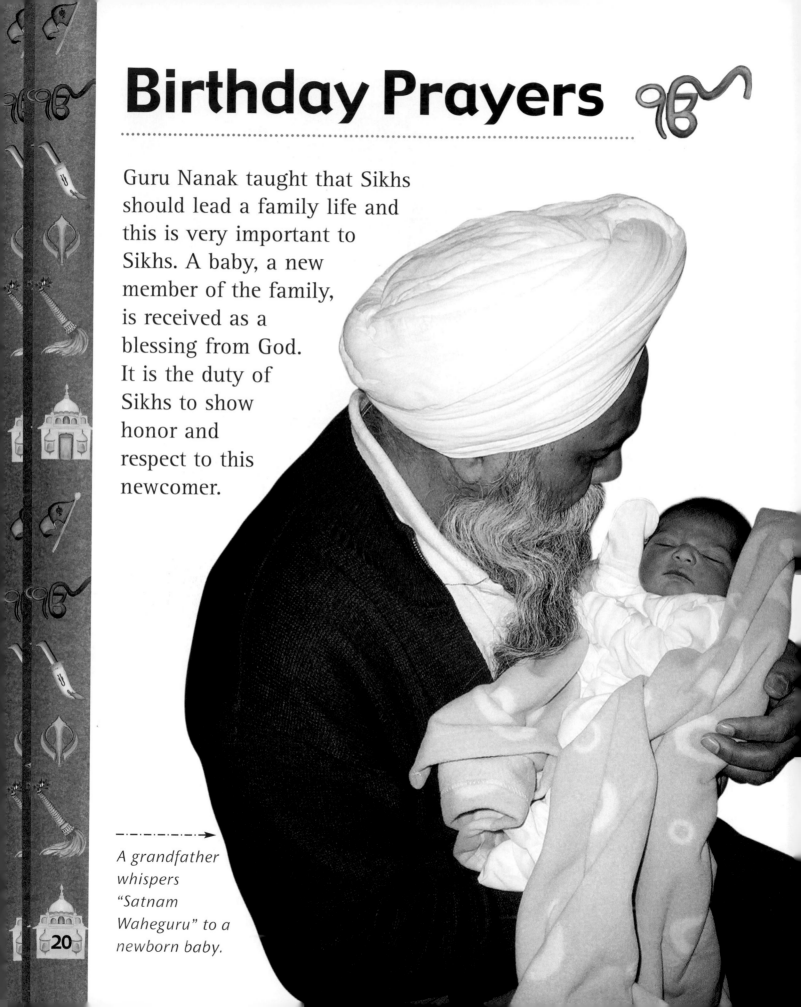

Guru Nanak taught that Sikhs should lead a family life and this is very important to Sikhs. A baby, a new member of the family, is received as a blessing from God. It is the duty of Sikhs to show honor and respect to this newcomer.

A grandfather whispers "Satnam Waheguru" to a newborn baby.

Naming a baby

When a baby is born, the words "Satnam Waheguru" (Truth is the name of the wonderful Lord) are whispered into its ear. A few weeks later, the parents take the baby to the gurdwara to thank God for its arrival. After the usual service, the granthi says a prayer:

"O God, by Your Grace,
this family has a gift of a child.
Please give us a letter for
the name of this child."

Then the granthi opens the Guru Granth Sahib at random. He reads out the first word on the left-hand page. The parents use the first letter of this word to choose a name for their baby. Once the name is chosen, it must be announced to the congregation in the presence of the Guru Granth Sahib.

Parents with their baby at his naming ceremony.

God has broken every barrier,
pain and sorrow swept away.
Blissful joy to all who know Him,
all to whom He gives His grace.

Joy abounds in all creation,
praise Him you who love your Lord,
God Almighty, perfect Master,
all pervading, everywhere.
God's eternal word has reached
us, chasing far our grief and care.
God is gracious, filled with
mercy, Nanak thus proclaims
this truth.

God has sent this wondrous gift;
born of grace, may his life be long.
Boundless the joy of his mother's
heart, when the child appeared
in her womb.

Born our son, born to adore,
faithful disciple of God.
His fate inscribed since time
began, now given for all to see.

About this prayer
This prayer is said at the naming ceremony by the granthi and a member of the child's family. Sikhs use it to thank God for a wonderful gift of a baby. They realize that life is worthless without God's blessing and grace.

Index

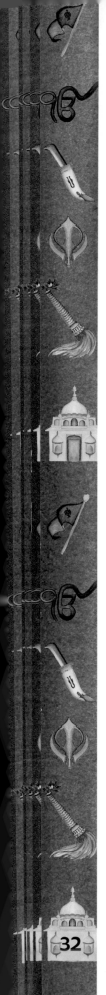